8298128R00056

Printed in Germany
by Amazon Distribution
GmbH, Leipzig